Why the Buffalo Walks Slowly and Treads Gently

Here is a story about a hardworking and faithful creature, popular in folk tales — the buffalo. This story comes from the East European country of Romania and tells us why the buffalo walks in the way it does.

Santhini Govindan

Illustrated By:
Prasonjit

PANDA
An imprint of Unicorn Books

In ancient times, the hare and the buffalo were constantly fighting each other because each believed he was the fastest creature around. The hare believed that his small lean legs were unbeatable, while the buffalo felt that his strong and muscular body, capable of great spurts of speed and power, gave him a position of supremacy. The two animals argued all the while about this matter and their enmity went on for years.

Finally, both animals grew tired of the constant fighting that sapped their energies and decided to resolve their long-standing dispute once and for all. The hare suggested that both rivals run a race to settle their quarrel. “Whoever wins the race will be proclaimed the fastest runner around,” Hare declared.

Buffalo was agreeable to this idea and a date and time for the race was fixed.

When the race began, Hare – laying his ears back flat against his head – began to race on his long, graceful legs. He ran swiftly and surely, and his feet barely touched the ground as they covered the distance. But large, powerful

Buffalo was more than a match for him. His body heaved as his hooves thundered over the ground. Soon, he gained on Hare and overtook him.

Hare, panting and breathless from the effort that he had put in, was dismayed when Buffalo raced ahead of him.

He kept running valiantly and determinedly, yet he knew that his small lean body could not match Buffalo's powerful one. But he could not bear the thought of losing such an important race and he thought desperately about what he could do to save the situation.

Then, as he watched huge and ungainly Buffalo racing along at a furious pace, he had a brainwave.

“Hey, Mr Buffalo! You had better be careful while you are thundering along. Haven’t you noticed that you are so huge and heavy that you are making the very Earth heave and shake with your giant steps?

Why, the Earth seems to be rocking under your feet and I am afraid that it will soon cave in and you will sink beneath it."

Buffalo was so alarmed when he heard this that he immediately stopped running and looked around in fear. After a while, he began to move again, but he took care to walk slowly and tread carefully so that the Earth would not rock beneath his feet anymore.

Hare chuckled in glee when he realised that his clever idea had worked so well and he ran ahead swiftly and won the race effortlessly.

Since that day Buffalo and Hare have never fought with each other again, but Buffalo is still full of fear that the Earth may open up if he thunders over it too quickly.

So he always takes care to walk slowly and tread very lightly and gently on the ground.